Earth Invasion By Space Aliens

Dr. Moses Oluwole

Copyright © 2020
All Rights Reserved
ISBN: 978-1-7356552-1-5

Dedication

I, Moses Oluwole, would like to dedicate this book to my Lord Jesus Christ, my loving darling Dr. Oladoyin Oluwole, family, friends, peers, and others who have helped me in my life's journey and given me the confidence and inspiration to express myself and my ideologies. Without them, I would never be in this position nor would I have attained my true potential.

Acknowledgment

I have to start by thanking my Supreme Teacher, Helper and Friend, God the Holy Spirit, for giving me the topic and all needed inspiration to carry out this noble project.

Secondly, thanks to my awesome darling, Doyin, who has been very supportive right from reading the early drafts to giving me wise counsel at every stage of the project up to the cover design. She was as important to this book getting done as I was. Thank you so much my beautiful darling.

About the Author

Hailing from Nigeria, I, Moses Oluwole, didn't have great aspirations in my early youth. I took life at face value and didn't have the opportunity to evaluate my life and think of greener pastures. However, despite my humble beginnings, through the grace of God, I managed to attain a Ph.D. in Industrial Chemistry from Germany and have been a Chemistry teacher for most of my life. I was able to attend the most competitive schools in my home country and abroad and I couldn't be more thankful to the Almighty for giving me this opportunity. Now, I wish to communicate my experiences to the nation's youth and enlighten them about the real challenges facing the USA and how, as a people, we can overcome them.

Introduction

A space mission goes out with 4 people and comes back with 4 people. However, one of them is not the same as before they left. An invasion of a foreign species begins to ravage the planet and Harlowe Thatch, the cause of the invasion, has to do all she can to try to fix what she has caused. Soon, however, Harlowe discovers that the invaders are unlike anything humanity has ever faced. In a bid to save her own life, Harlowe finds herself deeply embroiled in the fallout from her fateful space mission. With life on the planet hanging in the balance, there are no easy choices, but time is quickly running out.

Contents

DEDICATION	I
ACKNOWLEDGMENT	II
ABOUT THE AUTHOR	III
INTRODUCTION	IV
CHAPTER 1: THE QUIET INVASION	1
CHAPTER 2: CONTAGION	7
CHAPTER 3: THE ENEMY WITHOUT	22
CHAPTER 4: THE ENEMIES WITHIN	30
CHAPTER 5: THE SOLUTION	36
CHAPTER 6: THE AFTERMATH	61

Chapter 1: The Quiet Invasion

Harlowe felt the earth beneath her feet. She felt the pull of the planet on her body. She felt the warmth of sunlight and the touch of breeze on her face. She was home, finally.

Harlowe Thatch was an employee at Dublin Private Space Centre, a company that mostly conducted space missions for telecommunication companies in order to set up and maintain intricate satellites. Their recent trip, however, had involved an unusual commission. She had spent the month with three teammates, cultivating a special type of GMO that thrived best in zero gravity environments with cosmic rays to supplement their growth. However long missions in cramped spaces often led to cabin fever and conflict among the crew. While this mission had been mostly smooth sailing up until last week, Harlowe simply knew it was never going to last the whole mission.

Thomas Arnold and Regina Florentes, two of Harlowe's colleagues, were romantically involved by week two. Then by week four, it was revealed that Regina had also been previously involved with Dinar Pradesh, their fourth crew member, but it had been a secret liaison and... Harlowe had not bothered to learn the rest of the details really. Now that she was back home she would not have to deal with anyone else's personal life and she could go back to the regular schedule of Eat, Sleep, Work that she was used to. And it could not have come sooner. On the penultimate day of the mission she had heard a small but undeniable collision with the ship and, going out to check the damage caused by what she had supposed was space junk, she found a small spiky stone-like sphere. Reaching out to detach it from the ship, it had pierced through her suit suddenly and penetrated her fingers. The dull ache was still troubling her and the bickering between Regina and Thomas, reaching new heights, began to give her migraines. The mission ended just on time.

After debriefing the mission, she was finally allowed to drive home to the safety of the long-lost notion of Privacy. She nodded at colleagues who welcomed her back and stumbled out into the parking lot. Despite the asphalt underfoot she still felt the happy feel of Earthiness to everything around her. The familiar feel of the weight and solidness comforted her and while her head still hurt and the prickling in her index and ring finger still pulsed with the throbbing of her migraine, she looked forward to the sleep that would cure all the discomfort.

The sun was hot on the pitch and despite her simple cotton button-up blouse and plain suit pants, she felt beads of sweat on her head and neck. She unlocked Kingsley, the Code Name she had given her AutoCar, and fell into the seat, suddenly weak in the knees.

"Kingsley," she said, waking the AutoCar.

"Hello Harlowe. Welcome back. How was your trip?"

"Kingsley… pick up migraine medicine on the way home, please."

"My pleasure, Harlowe," responded the AutoCar computer. The small white compact had a fully transparent top half that allowed the sunlight through. But Harlowe felt herself getting sensitive to the light and dimmed the glass. With a flourish, it turned pitch black and a cool blue light illuminated the vehicle's interior.

The AutoCar's movement was nearly imperceptible as it took off. The world blurred slightly and the clammy sweat on Harlowe's brow made her even more uncomfortable. Her mouth started to fill with saliva, salty and profuse. She knew what it meant. Searching desperately, she found her coffee cup and threw up.

She felt the waves of nausea clench her stomach and had to cough and gag as something like spaghetti clogged her throat and nasal passage. It made her sick again and as she spat out the final bit of sick, she saw something long and white in her coffee cup that she could not identity. Just looking at the contents of the cup made her feel sick again, so she looked away and sealed it shut, utterly disgusted.

It was as if all the sickness in her was coming up and out of her body. The discomfort of the past two days exited her body in extraordinary fashion, and she breathed a sigh of relief but was shocked nonetheless.

"Uh... Kingsley," she said, once she regained her composure. "Um... take me back to the..." she was about to ask to go back to the office as the staff physician might have been able to assess why her symptoms had disappeared so strangely. It all felt very odd that she could simply be sick and then suddenly feel better. But feeling the exhaustion set into her bones, she realized that this could all wait until after the weekend.

"Kingsley," she said once more, "let's go straight home."

The AutoCar drove her quickly and when she entered her minimalistic high-rise apartment in the middle of the city, she washed her coffee cup in the sink, being sure to give it a good rinse. She could have sworn that she saw something move down in the drain, but she could not rely on her sleep-deprived brain at that point.

She went to her room, dimmed the window glass, and went to bed, falling into a deep, satisfying sleep almost immediately.

It was only until the neighbors let out a sudden blood-curdling scream that she woke up.

Chapter 2: Contagion

Harlowe ran out of her flat toward the noise. Once in the hallway she saw the Shaws, an elderly couple that lived next door running out of their loft and out toward the elevator. They left their door wide open and though they lived alone, there was still the sound of glass breaking and pans falling coming from where the kitchen in their unit ought to be.

Halowe could not resist the urge to investigate. She walked in cautiously and peered around the corner into the living room and to the kitchen beyond. She could not describe what she saw. A long, thin but strong white tentacle-like thing was protruding from the kitchen sink into the kitchen, whipping around the counter, pushing dishes and pots and pans off the drying rack.

She had never seen anything like it and her instinct to scream and recoil was only stayed by her training in the field that kept her nerves steady in unexpected situations.

The strength in whatever the thing was could not be denied. It was knocking and pushing against the sink and suddenly, it burst through in a flurry of water and little bits of food.

Harlowe backed away, fear choking her. It was a long tentacled creature, like a many-headed, worm rather than a squid or octopus. It had smooth, tentacles of varying sizes and lengths that were so white they were almost blue. It covered the width of the kitchen easily and used its appendages in agile movement. Pure strength. Completely unknown.

Then a strange thought occurred. The prick in her finger, a thing spaghetti, now a mere memory… Harlowe looked at her finger. The thin white sliver that had choked her. How she immediately felt better after being sick. Throwing the contents of the cup into the sink. The slight movement.

The idea that she had been infected by some alien species felt as absurd as it felt true. True. True. This being was alien. And Harlowe had brought it with her.

She felt confused and flustered. But she had to move.

Running out of the flat she slammed the door shut and hoped it would hold the creature back. She ran back into her loft, shouting as she did:

"Eva! Call Dinar!" Eva, her home management system computer responded with an affirmative beep and then the dial tone indicated that the call was being placed.

"Harlowe?" came Dinar's muffled voice over the loft intercom when he finally answered. His face appeared on her intercom interface screen, on the wall of the living room. He was in his bed, looking up at a similar screen.

"Dinar," she said, breathlessly, "something is happening and… I think I caused it."

"What?"

"There's a creature next door… I've never seen anything like it before and…"

"Wait, what?"

"I think I brought something home with me! Remember when I got pricked by that spiky bit of space debris? Remember how I got sick immediately after? I threw up on the way home and felt immediately better, no more migraine, no more aches or wooziness, nothing. And I threw it down the sink, it was in the drain system presumably and now there's some huge, weird creature in the neighbor's apartment..."

"Wow," Dinar was sitting up now and fully alert. "That's pretty crazy but also a huge leap... it could just be some unknown species that came from the ocean and into the drain system somehow... plus why are you calling me? Call Protective Services."

"No... I can't... Imagine if I'm right? I have a gut feeling. And if I call Protective Services and they do find out it's alien and I caused it, you know they'll quarantine me."

"Ok but that's for your safety as well as the safety of others, I mean..."

She flinched at the thought, but he was right. Reluctantly, she ended the call and then raised the Protective Services signal. There was still the muffled sound of the creature next door.

"What is the nature of your request?" asked Eva speaking on behalf of the Protective Services automated system.

"Call in the unknown species unit," said Harlowe.

It did not take long. Harlowe went out into the hallway cautiously. In a flurry of white hazmat suits and neon yellow water boots, they stormed the hallway and, without a word, followed Harlowe's finger, pointing at the door of the neighbors' apartment. They opened the door and what followed was a moment of frozen confusion.

"What…" said the man toward the front of the group. "I don't understand what that's supposed to be…"

"Is that supposed to be some kind of squid or something?" someone else asked. "What kind of pets are these people keeping?"

"It busted through the sink drain," Harlowe called to them as they inched forward. One of the officers of the service approached Harlowe.

"Do you know what this thing is," he asked.

"I haven't a clue, really, I just know that it's crazy strong."

"Have you been in contact with the creature?"

"No," she said, slightly hesitant as she did not want to reveal her theory if she did not have to.

"Where are the inhabitants of this apartment?"

"They ran away..."

He turned away and tapped his ComWatch. The watch on his wrist blinked blue and he spoke into it: "I need dispatch out in sector 895, we're looking for the inhabitants of square 44."

The watch blinked yellow to show that the message was received.

The sound of a sudden struggle broke out from the apartment and made Harlowe shake in fear.

"No, no, no," came a voice from inside the room. "Somebody shoot it!"

"Shoot where?" came another voice, panicked.

"Anywhere, damn it, shoot!"

The sound of a taser went off. Harlowe, despite herself, leant in to see. She could only spot the boots of one of the officers and hear the sound of a body being slammed into things.

"It bit me, god damn it…" said the first speaker before being cut off by a blow to the stomach or somewhere that cut off his air.

"Ma'am," said the man in the suit who had asked her questions, "I think you should leave; this is about to get ugly."

Harlowe did not hesitate or disagree. She ran into her apartment, picked up her purse and ran back out, ready to get as far away from this mess as she could.

Once in her AutoCar, she commanded Kingsley to drive. But halfway back to her office she felt it.

The headache. The pain in her finger. The nausea. It was starting again.

"Kingsley," she said, "drive faster."

*****

The car parked in front of Dublin and the sun beat down upon her body as she got out of the car and traversed the parking lot. It was as if the sunlight amplified her migraine tenfold.

Tripping her way into the building, she fumbled with her security card and made it as far as the elevator before a bout of dizziness overtook her and she felt her body lose all the strength needed to stand. She was surrounded by blackness and as she fell, she felt her body give in to the sickness that had decided to take hold of her.

The next thing she knew was the sound of a scanner firing up. She knew the sound well because she had carried out scans of her own many times, studying the body's response to certain treatments in Zero-G environments.

She opened her eyes and saw Dinar.

"Hey," she said. She was looking up at him, supine and semi-elevated, enough to see the room fully.

"Hey," said Dinar, voice quiet and worried. She grew aware of the fact that she was seeking his face through a film, and it dawned on her that he was wearing a hazmat suit. The room she was in was hermetically sealed. She was under quarantine.

"Oh no..." she whispered.

"Hey, hey," comforted Dinar, reaching out to wipe her brow of the cold sweat that beaded it. "You're all right. You're in good hands here. I want to find out what's going on with you and make sure you're all right. How do you feel?"

"I feel... like..." The wooziness set in once more. She felt the nausea build and Dinar responded right away, bringing her a basin.

It happened the same as before. Something stuck in her throat and came out. She did not look but she knew what she would see if she did.

Dinar set the basin aside and whispered quickly:

"Protective Services have reported a viscous flu outbreak among their staff and in some sections of the city. People are all reporting stings that then get followed up with flu-like symptoms. It's a sort of infection."

"But that means..."

"Yes. It's some sort of invasion by a foreign species. But now that I have a sample," he nodded toward the basin, "I can identify what exactly it is and bring them proper information."

"Ok," she nodded. She started to get up as, just like before, she felt completely restored.

"No, no," chided Dinar. "We have to scan you. You said you were sick before and you got sick again. What's to say you aren't hosting more parasites?"

Harlowe felt herself grow a little faint at the thought once more.

She sat still as Dinar went over to the basin. He used a pair of medical tongs to pick up a short, thin, white-blueish worm-like creature with small tentacles of varying lengths extending from its body.

Dinar placed it carefully in a small container and he began to close it. It was in that moment that the stringy little thing began to writhe and wrestle, flipping over and thrashing this way and that. It pushed against the cover that Dinar was fumbled with, shocked at the sudden movement.

Harlowe screamed. That thing had been in her! She felt her skin crawl with disgust.

Dinar finally got the container closed and the worm continued to thrash with a surprising strength. Dinar grabbed a medical glove quickly and tied it around the container to keep the lid further in place. Finally, he placed the contained on a mobile table top and let out a sigh of either relief or shock, Harlowe could not tell which. Dinar turned to face her, eyes popping out of his skull from behind the film.

"I felt it push back," he said, shocked.

"I saw," said Harlowe, quietly, choked by a mounting panic.

"What the hell is that thing?" asked Dinar.

Harlowe shook her head in confusion.

"I need you to get every trace of those things out of me."

Dinar nodded. He went over to the overhead scanner and dragged it over to her bed.

"Stay still," he said, his voice trembling but still a little reassuring.

He ran the scanner with a steady hand.

"Dinar..." said Harlowe, her breath coming in quicker and more uneven by the second.

"It's ok, I'm here, we're just gonna finish this scan, ok."

She nodded and took deep breaths, forcing herself to be calm.

"All right, all done," he announced a minute later. "So, we'll just let it analyse the information. It'll be fine, we'll figure out how to deal with it and we'll fix this."

He walked over to her bed and held her hand with one hand while brushing her hair back with the other.

"So... aside from, uh, possible alien parasite infection, how's it been being back?"

Harlowe laughed weakly.

"Uh, I've had a restful night for the first time in a long time. Nobody fighting in the background..."

"Ugh..." Dinar winced. "Don't even remind me... I don't know what came over me, we were just always together and she just... she acted like it was just fine to prance around as if I didn't have any feelings, as if we never had anything, as if she hadn't kept it quiet because she thinks she can do better... I just..."

"I get it, I've always got it, just didn't want to have to be around it."

"Oh God, I must be the worst person, here I am complaining about --"

"No, it's good, it feels like something normal. This should have been a return to normal, everyday Earth life."

Dinar fell silent. The scanner beeped. Dinar hesitated. He gave Harlowe's hand a squeeze before going over to the tablet attached to the overhead scanner. It was the size of a school desktop.

Dinar was quiet for a while, scanning documents, flipping through screens. Harlowe was tempted to ask him to show her the screen too but she refrained and simply focused on her breathing and tried to block out the sound of the worm in the corner rattling around in his container or the growing creepy-crawly feeling in her stomach and under her skin.

"So..." said Dinar, finally. "It's clear what we need to do, more or less. The sting site is housing a sort of 'Queen' insect that is releasing eggs, one at a time it seems as there's only evidence of two foreign entities. So, I just need to remove the insect and the gestating egg that's in your blood stream and finding its way into your digestive system. Your body is savvy enough to recognize it as foreign when it starts to get too big. What's alarming, really, is the growth rate."

"Dinar I don't care about that right now, please just get them out of me!"

"Oh, ok, yes, I'll call Colin in to deal with it." He came to her side. "You'll be fine, ok, I can all but guarantee it. This is just a small parasite like any other invasive species. This one just happens to have foreign origins. It'll be all right."

"That's... that's actually reassuring. Make sure to call Protective Services with this information so that they can start taking up the procedure for the others who have been infected."

"Aye, aye." He smiled at her and Harlowe actually felt relief.

Chapter 3: The Enemy Without

It was a quick procedure and an easy fix in the end.

Harlowe was taken care of in a few hours. They had a Queen, a larva and baby worm to examine, all in separate specimen cases.

Harlowe stepped into the bathroom of her examination room in order to wash her face and brush her teeth, using the sealed toiletry set on the counter. When she came out, fresh faced and breathed, she saw a newcomer, a fairly unassuming man but for her sharp eyes behind a pair of spectacles.

"Harlowe Thatch?" asked the man. She nodded. "Dean Jr. Kane, Protective Services dispatch. I'm aware that you are basically our Patient Zero?"

She nodded once more.

"You being an individual with a great deal of responsibility, working in space as you do, I would expect you to have been more aware of protocols, Ms. Thatch. Can I ask why you brought yourself here instead of to a proper containment unit at Protective Services?"

"I don't believe I need to answer that, we're all aware that Dublin has identical if not superior technology and capability…"

"Ms. Thatch, a matter of public safety is not to be handled by private companies. Your buddies may have given you a clean bill of health but I'm afraid we need to assess that for ourselves."

She did not resist the assertion despite the fact that his scolding tone annoyed her to no end.

"Then lead the way, Mr. Kane."

Dean opened the door for her and they walked down the hall together passing laboratories and empty examination rooms.

"Do you like working at Dublin," Dean asked suddenly.

"Oh, yeah, sure. It's a workplace like any other workplace after you get past the glamor of space but it's still pretty cool."

Dean seemed poised to ask another question but then a loud noise, all too familiar, erupted from behind them. Harlowe whipped around on full alert. She heard a shriek and then:

"Did you see how fast it grew?"

"They're really strong, I think we should--" but then the speech was cut short. A loud thud shook the door and the small window in the door was suddenly splattered with blood and what looked like small blobs of flesh...

It was brain matter, Harlowe realized in sudden horror.

She could not hold back her scream of horror and it was only matched by Dean's own yell of anguish.

Frozen in place, Harlowe could hardly force herself to move as her body locked up in terror, as though the bone were made of metal and the joints ceased to exist. It was only when Dean dragged her by her shirt and elbow that she followed, looking over her shoulder, hearing the sounds of horror behind her.

She ran as fast as her legs could carry her, faster than Dean, even, who spoke into ComWatch, calling in for backup.

"Go to your car," Dean ordered. Harlowe did not hesitate. She ran out into the parking lot. She could not remember where she had parked. She shouted out into the parking lot: "Kingsley!" and continued running. The car would find her soon enough. She continued running as far away from the building as she could.

Her AutoCar drove to meet her and she hopped in, ordering Kingsley to make the windshields transparent and to call Dublin Security.

"Hello?" It was a middle-aged woman who Harlowe more or less recognized. She was of a very sturdy build and had a friendly demeanour.

"Hello, I'm calling to report a level 5 disruption on floor 3. Someone was killed by an alien species. Protective Services have been called but the whole building should be on lockdown. These creatures have immense strength, they are infectious parasites that breed at a rapid rate and human contact should be limited at all costs."

"Yes, ma'am," said the Security guard, and she then transmitted a replay of Harlowe's message over the Emergency megaphone throughout the entire Dublin complex.

Soon enough there were people running out of the building and into their cars. Protective Services emerged soon enough too.

Harlowe felt her breathing for the first time. Her heart was nearly throbbing out of her chest and her breathing was rapid and shallow. She trembled as she began to wonder if Dinar had been the one in that laboratory. She could not bear the thought, but she called him to find out.

"Harlowe, what's up?" asked a groggy-sounding Dinar.

She felt her chest choke with the lack of breath and the tears of relief she felt seeing Dinar's scrunched up face on the call.

"There was another attack another of the creatures…"

"Really? At Dublin?"

"Yes."

"Damn it… who…? Do you know who… wait…"

There was a loud thumping in the background. Dinar pressed his ear to the wall.

"Oh my God," he mumbled. "It's like… it's like it's directly against the wall… I…"

But suddenly in a burst of drywall, splinters, and dust, a hole punched straight into Dinar's headboard and into his skull, splattering red mist all over the camera.

Harlowe sat frozen and terrified as she watched the wormlike creature punch through the wall further and terrorize the family next to Dinar's apartment at the same time.

"Kingsley… drive to Protective Services headquarters."

The car took off, speeding down the streets, even as Harlowe saw chaos break out around her as people ran screaming from the Dublin building. Security and Protective Services would do what they could. Harlowe would be of no use there. But she felt sure that she could help Protective Services get to the bottom of finding a solution to what Harlowe felt was an invasion of an aggressive alien species. She was a skilled biologist and she would be of service in the safety of their offices.

As the car drove, however, Harlowe felt her body tense and her jaw lock up. It was sudden and unbidden. She felt herself suddenly lose control of her body and even her mouth in what was the most hideously unnerving experience of her life.

Her mouth opened and the words came out, but they were not hers.

"Kingsley," she heard herself say. "Take me back to Dublin."

"Ok, Harlowe," Kingsley replied.

No! She thought to herself. This is not what I want! How did that happen? Why can't I move?

The car stopped as soon as it legally could and drove her back to the hell that was unfolding.

Harlowe watched on with horror as her body unlocked and she walked toward the building that she had just fled. People were jumping into their cars and a few Protective Services trucks were parked. Men in hazmat suits carrying guns lined up in front of the building, ushering individuals out and into a nearby truck, no doubt to check them for infection. Harlowe wanted to scream for help. She wanted to stop her body from doing what it was doing. But she could not. It was as if her body was being controlled by something unknown. Whatever it was, it was not her.

Chapter 4: The Enemies Within

Harlowe's feet carried her around to the side entrance of the main building, away from the men in hazmats. She flashed her ID, or rather, her body did and in she went.

She wanted to scream. She wanted to claw her face off. She wanted to do anything to stop this unfamiliar horror. But instead her body carried her to the staircase and led her up to the third floor.

It played out in a sort of slow motion. She went into the corridor and found the large worm with its many appendages moving independently of one another, hulking in the middle of the dimly lit hall. Normally there were bright fluorescents, but lights had been damaged, no doubt in the rampage the worm went on as Harlowe had seen enough to know that these creatures were particularly skilled at destruction.

She felt her body go rigid and tried with everything in her to turn around and run away. But, as though trapped in a dream experiencing sleep paralysis, she felt herself trapped in a body that no longer belonged to her. Standing in front of the worm as it occupied the entire hallway, she felt herself prepare for death. It was a good ten paces away but as her body led her to stand in place, the worm stopped thrashing and, if it had eyes, Harlowe would have guessed that it was looking at her. Instead, it simply became still.

Then, with a sudden and swift movement, it rushed toward her, tentacles of varying lengths outreached, and it stung her, at least ten times, in ten different places.

The waves of terror, disgust, anger and pain that washed through her rendered her nearly senseless as she struggled with all her might to move, to run, to escape from this indignity of being made an incubator for these disgusting parasites.

The confusion and fear led way to clarity. Something in these worms had left a mark on her brain and had learned how to turn her into a zombie. These animals could sense one another and were focused merely on self-replicating, breeding, as much as possible. They could control their hosts, even after seemingly being flushed out of the host's system.

This creature had taken over her body.

It had taken over her mind.

Unbidden but somehow refreshingly hers, a single tear flowed out of her eye as the animal pierced her skin.

She somehow found herself back out in the parking lot.

She had never felt so violated in her life. She wanted to self-immolate. She wanted death then and there. Her body was slowly becoming hers again, but it did not matter. The stings all over her body were enough reminder of the invaders inside. As she walked, shell-shocked and self-loathing, she soon came across a Protective Services field officer. When he looked up at her, she began to mouth the word: "Help" but it did not come out, it was a mere whisper.

She squeaked the word out as she moved woodenly toward him, her face taut with disbelief and terror, trying to push the words out, gaining more and more air as she did until her voice cracked like a broken bone into the air and her scream tore through her throat: "HELP! Help! Please, help!"

The man rushed over to her, hazmat suit shuffling loud plastic. He grabbed her: "Are you ok, Miss?"

She was not. She lost all the stiffness in her body only to collapse into a pool of unwilling limbs that could no longer withstand the stress of being upright.

"I've been... they've... I'm infected," she whispered. The man in his suit leaned in to hear her. "I'm infected, stung all over. I'm the one from the ship, I'm the one who brought them here first. I touched the egg... I touched the egg."

"Egg?" asked the man. "What egg? What egg?"

But Harlowe could not answer. The sun beating down on her became unbearable. Her head felt as though it were increasingly on fire. As her adrenaline wore down, she began to feel the symptoms of the infection, ten times worse than before. The anguish of looking out into the light cause her to curl in on herself. Each and every sound around her was a shock to the system; she covered her ears against it. As the world became dizzy and uneven, she felt sweat collect on her brow and threaten to empty her out like a rag being wrung dry.

"Ok, let's take her to the truck," said the man in the suit who was apparently joined by another. Soon Harlowe was on a gurney and being rushed into the nearest First Aid truck. They stripped her body, and someone winced at the lacerations all over her skin.

Then came the anaesthesia.

Chapter 5: The Solution

Harlowe awoke and felt her stomach churn. For the second time she was laid out on her back, totally helpless, with little control over her own body.

When had she become this person? She had always been strong-willed. A fighter. And yet here she was, victim to a worm, over and over again.

"Oh, there you are," came a kind voice interrupting her inner turmoil. It was a young doctor with a kind face, perhaps in his late twenties.

"I'm Dr. Neil O'Bran. How are you feeling?"

"Violated," answered Harlowe honestly.

"I can only imagine."

"Dr. O'Bran," she said hesitantly as he picked up the Charts Tablet that held patients' information. He swiped this way and that pensively for a second and looked up to give her his attention.

"Yes?" he said.

"For your other patients around the city, it is important to know that the creatures may be able to influence individuals against their will."

"How do you mean?" he asked, puzzled.

"The reason why I got... stung so many times... I lost control of my body, the animal... it somehow took over my body and it... it drew me to it. It took over my body."

"I don't understand..."

"It somehow had left some kind of chemical agent or parasite or something that controlled my brain and forced my body to walk inside Dublin and up to the worm so that it could add more queens into my body."

The doctor looked shocked.

"I think…" continued Harlowe, "I might be of use to the Protective Services. We might be able to make an exchange. I can offer my field biology and alien life skills to help understand how this worm took over my body and then, maybe even reverse engineer the chemical signals they use to find each other -- because I simply have to assume that I was pulled toward the nearest parasite due some sort of pheromonal response, some heightened sense of needing to 'mate' that can subsume free will. So perhaps we can use that to draw the worms in and lead them to a deservedly bloody demise."

Dr. O'Bran looked almost insultingly surprised at Harlowe's direct thought-process and intelligence.

"Wow," he said. "That's brilliant! But… you said an 'exchange?' What would you want in return?"

"I want to be quarantined in the biggest, strongest cage you can find. I do not EVER want what happened to me this morning to happen again."

"I understand. I'll make the call."

"Wait. One other thing. I am the one who brought the aliens back. There's an egg on the ship. It gave me the first sting. You should… send someone to get it." Harlowe did not want to go anywhere near Dublin, perhaps ever again. Dr. O'Bran looked taken aback and slightly horrified. The idea that Harlowe was the reason for all this… she did not expect anyone to look favorably upon her. But the doctor maintained his composure for the most part.

"Got it," he said. He then stepped out to make a phone call.

*****

Harlowe felt a new sense of purpose and strength course through her veins. She was going to get her revenge for this foul thing inside of her. Now sitting in a medic van, she sat next to Dr. O'Bran in the back of the truck in silence. Every now and then flashes of unwanted images came before her mind's eye. Coughing up the first worm. Being drawn toward the worm and pierced. Dinar. Poor, poor Dinar. And the words: "All your fault" floated all neon-bright hatred in her mind.

She shook herself. She could not think about it. If she did, she would not recover. Dinar had been her friend. The emptiness left by his death could not yet be felt because its vastness was still being uncovered. She chose, instead to focus on the possible chemical agents that could have manipulated her to lose control of her body. It was a short drive to the containment facility where there was a great deal of commotion and, oddly enough, construction noises. "They are reinforcing the containment units," Dr. O'Bran explained as they walked through the entrance hall of the Protective Services Regional Base. Grey marble underfoot and vast cathedral ceilings soared above. Harlowe's footsteps echoed reassuringly along the marble, telling her that she had control of her body, that she was moving in the right direction, that she was on the right path.

She was soon installed in small laboratory. While it looked like an examination room, it was also outfitted with a research area and several test kits and note-taking devices. In fact, it looked like a coroner's office. And for some reason, Harlowe felt like a dead woman walking. She looked at the walls with doubt.

"No worries," explained Dr. O'Bran. "It's got steel sheets between the concrete blocks, the walls can withstand a great deal of pressure. Once we're locked it, we're locked in."

"Ok." Harlowe sat at the table present. "Ok. So, we need to take some blood samples, do some brain scans, and get to the bottom of what it is that is or was in me that took over my body."

"All right. Ms. Thatch… can I call you Harlowe?"

"Sure…"

"You can call me Neil," he said, helpfully

"Thanks," said Harlowe, chuckling, "I was trying desperately to remember your name."

"Well now you know," he said gently. "So, Harlowe, let's examine you."

It was a very strange and almost inappropriate feeling to find Neil's tone and proximity as he guided her to the examination table appealing. She felt a small flutter in her stomach as he guided her gently, hand hovering near the small of her back, onto the table. She was still somewhat unsteady on her feet and she resisted the urge to reach out to him for stabilization, as that would likely undermine her future efforts to regain dominance in the lab, something she knew she would require as she had dealt with alien life forms before and having Neil second-guess her would inconvenience the situation entirely.

It was a funny train of thought all together, but the final resolution made Harlowe chuckle quietly at the absurdity.

"What?" asked Neil, wanting in on the joke.

"Nothing," said Harlowe quickly, laying back on the elevated examination table.

Harlowe unbuttoned her top button in order to give the scanner better access as the buttons were metallic clasps which she knew could interfere with readings every now and then. She felt Neil's eyes on her fingers although he tried to be discrete and though she did not mind, once more she was struck with the absurdity of such thoughts in the middle of such chaos and tragedy.

"So…" said Neil, quietly, adjusting his glasses, "I'm just going to scan your brain quickly with a triple-layer scan, should take ten minutes, so please sit very still so that we can get a good working model of your neural pathways. We can then print out a couple 3D copies and synthesize some of the chemicals that might be triggering the strange behaviors you described."

"Ok, ready," said Harlowe.

"All right. I'm going to ask you some questions and give you some trigger words."

"Sure."

He pulled up another tall rolling scanner, hooked like a hair dryer at a salon. It was black with blue light shining down on Harlowe's face. She looked up at the soft light and stayed still.

"Ok, so can you say some baseline words, please," said Neil.

"My name is Harlowe Thatch. 1, 2, 3, 4. A, B, C, D."

"Very good. Now, let's get an emotional reading. Describe this morning."

"I..." Harlowe hesitated. "I witnessed my good friend getting killed. And then I was... raped... by an invader species that I brought to the planet." She felt her emotions shatter into a million pieces, all too small and scattered to be felt properly.

"That's..." said Neil. "We've got a good reading of that. I'm..."

"What's next?" asked Harlowe, releasing a heavy breath at the same time. She did not want to dwell.

"Can you picture things in your mind?"

"Yes - can't everyone?"

"No actually, there's a significant number who cannot. Anyway, let's picture an apple."

Harlowe thought of a red apple.

"Ok, now a cat."

Harlowe thought of a black cat with green, feminine eyes.

"Ok, now, think of the invader species."

Harlowe flinched as she saw the worm extend its tentacles to her body. She felt it pierce her skin again. She saw it thrashing through the wall into Dinar's skull. She saw it rip through the sink and into her neighbors' apartment. She saw the worm everywhere. She felt as though she might be choking on one in that moment.

"Ok, that's enough, Harlowe," said Neil. "Harlowe!"

She was threatening to crack. Neil grabbed her shoulders. She looked at him tremulously.

"Hey," he said, his voice breaking. "Hey. Just focus on the light. Don't think about anything, just… focus on the light and… we'll be ok."

She nodded, not trusting herself to speak.

Suddenly, there was a buzzing noise throughout the building and the loudspeakers came on saying:

"Attention. Preliminary findings show that the new invasive life-forms have some degree of intelligent behavior. They are not merely animals but showing signs of purpose and organization."

In that moment, Harlowe was sure the scanner pictured a whole storm of activity in her brain.

*****

It was a tedious process of trial and error over the next three hours to discover and isolate the chemical compound in her brain but as they scanned and examined it, the computer kept insisting that while the compound was foreign, it was not organic. The print-out explained that there was an intentionality and order uncommon in organic material. It was deemed "Man-Made" but also "Unknown" in origin.

"Do you think…" said Harlowe, "it's possible for these creatures to have created this?"

"Maybe…" said Neil. "It seems so unlikely though…"

"They are aliens after all… no reason why their intelligence should resemble ours in any way."

"I wish I could get my hands on a fully grown one... some of our teams have tried but they can only work with the baby worms, they're so hard to subdue once they get big... and the way they have been growing and rampaging... It's hard for us to keep up..."

"I'll feel free to excuse myself when you get your specimen."

"Oh, of course..." said Neil, apologetically.

"So... let's have a look at this chemical then," said Harlowe.

There was a large blank wall behind them that Harlowe dragged the tablet image to project onto. Swivelling around to the screen and holding the tablet in order to control the image, Harlowe examined the microscopic view of what it was that had taken root in her brain. Suddenly, however, before she could proceed, she saw a small icon pop up in the bottom right of the screen showing a question mark.

"Oh, you should open that," said Neil, reaching across to tap the tablet screen before she could.

It opened a small chat box that read: 6 viewers.

"What--" began Harlowe.

"Six other teams in the building are looking on at the work too. We're sharing the information we uncover in order to expedite a solution."

"Ok."

"If you tap the little icon with the group of people in the chat box, they can join the conversation." Again, he did not wait for Harlowe to act but went ahead and tapped. She was slightly annoyed but suddenly the faces of six pairs of people popped up in a bottom section of the projected screen.

"Hello," said Harlowe. Neil waved.

"What's up, Neil?" said one of the young men on the screen while the others nodded in greeting.

"Hey," said Neil. "We're just about to examine Harlowe's brain scan. There are some unknown fluids and chemicals that are left over in her system. They have a sort of zombie parasite effect where the parasite controls the host for its own Darwinist purposes."

"Christ..." came a whisper from a young Asian girl.

"Yeah, it's pretty nasty," said Harlowe. "According to the AI assessment, it's an inorganic compound. Looking at it now... it's... wait..." She paused to zoom the image in better. There was a collective gasp.

"If I didn't know any better..." began Neil.

"That's like... a freaking circuit board!" said one of the viewers.

"How is that possible?" asked another.

On the screen was a small tadpole-like creature with a spinning tail, very mechanical in nature with fixed movement. It was transparent with a thin, plastic-like casing. Inside of its little body was what was uncannily like a circuit board.

"It's like a nano-robot," said Harlowe. "It's got some translucent casing, but it's clearly got some sort of orderly circuitry in it... how is that really possible?"

"Wow," said Neil. "I cannot begin to understand how something so seemingly destructive and animalistic would even come to create something so small and subtle... and adaptable - they've likely never come across a human brain, we'd have heard about such a creature..."

"I've got my hands on a subject," said the Asian girl. "We've ascertained that they grow exponentially when hydrated - that's why they thrive in bodies and in drains - but they're still manageable when they're new-borns. I'm going to test for these bots - they could come from the queens, the worms themselves, the egg or all of them. Ms. Thatch, you're the only one to have been in physical contact with the egg, right?"

"Yes," replied Harlowe. "From what I know, none of the team members ever touched it and I was so sick when I left Dublin, I hardly remembered to take it out of the ship. It's been in a sealed container ever since I found it."

"And," said Neil, suddenly, "these may not be the only lifeforms out there, these animals may not even be the creators, despite whatever intelligence has been discovered in them. The nanobots may be the creation of a more intelligent species on whichever planet they come from. The worms could just be the equivalent of a bacteria or a moth that came along with the original message..."

"Basically, we need to check out the egg," concluded Harlowe.

"Yes. I got someone to search for it; it was in the queue for sanitization last I checked."

"We need it now," insisted Harlowe. She needed answers. She needed to know what was inside of her. Again, she felt her skin crawling like her body was not hers and at times, although she knew they were far too small to feel, she still could not help but imagining the invasive little nanobot worms scraping against her skull. She shook herself out of it and brought herself back to the proceedings at hand.

"In the meantime, she said, "which of you guys is best with simulation engineering?" She looked at the twelve faces on her screen.

"I think Joe is really the guy," said Neil. Joe, a dark and handsome young man nodded modestly.

"I think it would be fitting to see if you can reverse engineer the nanobot in order to control the worms. I don't know how far along you guys have come with breaking down the worms' anatomies..." She looked at the young Asian girl for information.

"It's been slow work as all of our AI is based on earth organisms, but we've understood a great deal, including ascertaining their brains. They have two, in fact, one dedicated to motor functions, a very small thing that then unites something like a nervous system. Then another that regulates needs and reward systems in order to fill those needs. So, hydration, sustenance, respiration, and so on. As far as intelligence, while we have been able to see them use tools, learn quickly, show creative thinking, and even communicate with one another using their tentacles to make elaborate signs; our biggest deterrent for knowing whether or not they have human-like intelligence is the fact that they don't like to do anything even when they suspect they are being observed. Time, so far, has been our biggest obstacle, we just haven't had enough time and their spread and growth rate is prohibitive to more careful study."

"Ok," said Harlowe. "What's your name, please?"

"Skye."

"Ok, Skye, I'm Harlowe. This is good progress given that it's been merely a few days. I would say let's work on trying to ensure we find a way to control the bots that took over my motor-control and do the same to them in order to get them away from people."

"The egg's ready!" said Neil suddenly, looking down at his watch. "The custodian is bringing it now. Guys," he said to the people on the screen. "I'll send a quick task breakdown based on Harlowe's ideas. I think it may be the least harmful way forward since we know how hard they fight when we try to use force. The less casualties, the better."

There was a brief exchange of goodbyes before the call ended.

"Now." Neil turned to Harlowe, matter-of-factly. "That was an excellent set of ideas, Harlowe. But now that we know for sure that you have foreign machines in your brain, I think you have to be cleansed before we can continue any further."

"Wait, what?"

"I can't be sure that you're not going to do something unpredictable with those things in your head. We have to get you clean. You will have to be given over to a doctor for help."

"No... but... I want to help, I'm more useful --"

"Clean. You have to be in control of yourself if you wish to help us."

"I..." she could not come up with a valid argument. He was right of course. She did not know if the egg would influence her in anyway, not when there was irrefutable proof that her brain was swimming with nanobots that could control her.

"Harlowe..." said Neil, reaching out to hold her hand. "I'm sorry. I feel like you and I are alike, I know for sure I would want to be here helping instead of being laid out on a hospital bed."

"Yeah," she whispered. "It's cool though," she said, faking a casual tone. "It's the responsible thing to do. I'm actually shocked everyone is being so nice to me, given that I'm the one who caused all of this." Tears threatened to sting her eyes, but she blinked them away. She knew once she started, she would never stop. The death toll was climbing by the minute. And Dinar...

"Hey," said Neil, seeing the anguish break out over her face. He grabbed her by the shoulders quickly. "Hey, it's going to be all right."

"This is my doing..."

"No. It could have happened to anyone... this egg was on a collision course with Earth all along, your ship just intercepted it. It may have burnt up in the atmosphere, it may not. There are too many variables to know for sure whether this was inevitable or not but you can't blame yourself either way."

There was a knock on the door.

A man entered the room, pushing a rolling tray with a clear box. Inside was a grapefruit-sized white ball with sharp spikes protruding out of it.

It was so white that it was almost blue. Harlowe felt fear shudder through her, seeing the thing that has caused so much anguish. And as she trembled, she saw the egg begin to rattle. At first, she thought that she was imagining it. But then it rattled faster and faster, even as she shivered faster and faster too.

With a building bile, she felt herself being controlled again. She felt her body stop belonging to her.

In the corner of her eye, the egg rattled and glowed blue-white, pulsing. The custodian stepped back from it, completely frightened and Neil himself was stiff in shock, not sure what was happening or what to do for a moment.

And suddenly a hand that was not hers reached out for her tablet and tapped on the intercom button. With quick-moving fingers, she typed something even she could not understand. The computer AI responded in a quick flash of blue-on-white binary and then suddenly Harlowe saw her face projected onto the wall with a small banner along the bottom of the screen reading: Worldwide AI Emergency Broadcast. This was the worldwide emergency system that all computer items had for disasters. It had happened so fast that neither Neil nor the custodian could do anything and by the time it was done, they were all too confused to do anything.

Harlowe felt shock and horror but could not move her face in order to project it. In total confusion she watched as her projected face opened her mouth and spoke. The voice was deeper than her normal speaking voice, but it was still her voice. It frightened her to see it. "Humans of Earth," said the voice. "This is the mouthpiece of the Urr. We are an extra-terrestrial species. We found shelter in the one you call Harlowe Thatch. She was the unfortunate carrier of our species. We send out hybrid species crossed with artificial intelligence on colonizing missions but because you are the first intelligent species we have ever come across, it took some time for us to understand fully that you are not just simple creatures. We then had to study the one you call Harlowe Thatch in order to understand how you communicate in order to deliver this message.

"We have caused some damage, for which we are very sorry. This is an AI glitch that has backfired. Unfortunately, we are a species that requires living hosts in order to help us carry on our seed. We make use of our hosts for more than just breeding purposes as they tend to have better control of their appendages than the females of our species do and therefore make for good working tools. We did this naturally for millennia throughout our evolution before becoming skilled in computing, robotics, and artificial intelligence that was more efficient in controlling hosts. However, our species has a strict code of ethics that forbids harming beings with strong signs of intelligence. We have crossed that line and beg forgiveness. All of our hybrids are set to self-destruct in around one Earth minute. We will mark this planet as off-limits for future colonization and welcome the possibility of meeting you one day in the stars. Thank you. Goodbye."

The broadcast ended.

Then, as though all the breath had escaped from her body all at once, Harlowe felt her body become hers once more. Suddenly she felt sick again and threw up into the nearest trashcan. In it, she suspected, was the last of the foreign bodies, leaving her.

She looked up to see Neil and the custodian staring at her. She then looked at the egg. It pulsed a brighter and brighter blue before suddenly disintegrating into a cloud of blue that settled into a grey, ashen dust on the bottom of the container. There were screams echoing throughout the building.

The Intercom burst to life and the AI Emergency broadcast revealed: "All foreign lifeforms have been destroyed. The invasion threat has ended."

Chapter 6: The Aftermath

It took some convincing to believe that the solution could come so easily. In a fit of tears and depression, Harlowe came to terms with the past few days slowly in the next few hours as Neil examined her for any residual damage. There was none and her scans all showed her as clean and healthy as the day she left Earth on her mission.

Neil brought her some soup to eat and then left her alone with her thoughts. He looked slightly frightened of her, if anything. She did not blame him. She felt frightened of herself.

Soon after, she called a car to carry her to a hotel as her apartment was damaged in the aftermath of that first attack.

She spent two days, locked away, crying to herself.

The third day she decided to brave the outside world only to be accosted by a ravenous group of reporters just outside the hotel. In a panic, she ran back inside and up to her room. This time she did not leave for a week.

At one point someone had broken through security to come to her room door and she hid in her bathroom until the knocking and yelling was stopped by a bellboy.

Finally, on the 11th day she heard a knock.

"Ms. Thatch," said the voice quietly.

"No reporters," she shouted, viciously.

"Yes, yes Ms. we've kept them away just like you asked. But, there's a Mr. O'Bran here and he said he's a high-level researcher with Protective Services and I wouldn't bother you only... we're not allowed to refuse orders that have to do with public health and you being the mouthpiece for a dangerous invasive species and all..."

"Oh, for heaven's sake," came a curt whisper. "You really had to go there," snapped the quiet voice. It was Neil, of course.

Harlowe went to the door and opened it enough to peek through. The chain still held the bolt fast.

"Hey," said Neil. "I brought soup," he said, holding up a brown paper bag, bulging with two containers.

Harlowe opened the door.

"Hey," she said, once he was inside and far enough from her not to smell her breath. She had not done her best in maintaining her hygiene during her time alone.

"How have you... been...?" he asked, distracted by the mess of clothing and dirty dishes scattered around the living room of her hotel suite.

"Um... great..." she said, quickly scooping up the bra, jeans, shirt and underwear scattered on the floor. She was currently wearing nothing but her bathrobe, like every other day. "I'll be right back," she said quickly.

She ran to her room and dumped the clothes on the bed then ran into the bathroom to wash her face, brush her teeth, do something about her hair, and put on her bra, jeans, and t-shirt before going back out.

"Hey," she said with a fake chirpiness to hide her true mood.

"How have you been?" asked Neil.

"You know... good as I can be. Avoiding the reporters and the news."

"You shouldn't."

"I don't want to know how many people I've killed and injured; how many I've left orphaned..."

"I... see... and while that is playing into the news-cycle, mostly people are just excited that you discovered life in the universe. That was you. You discovered intelligent life!"

"What? Is that how people are talking about it?" She sat across from him. "I hardly discovered so much as bumbled..."

"It doesn't matter, plenty of scientists have stumbled across their greatest work. You, Harlowe Thatch, will go down in history as having discovered the fact that we, humans, are not alone in the universe. And while it's scary to know that, you've also discovered that benevolence among sentient creatures is also something we can look forward to."

Harlowe was confused. She had been certain that she was going to be on the receiving end of every lawsuit, every kind of blame, endless hatred... She had never anticipated for a second that anyone would thank her for her blunder.

"But... I mean... People are dead..."

"Yes. They are. But pretty much most of the incidents of violence excepting a few were situations of mortal peril for both parties. Only one was coming out alive in these situations and if we're talking about equally sentient beings... I may be too clinical, but I can understand the situation from both ends. It's not pleasant but a lot of people went down fighting. There are very few completely innocent deaths. So... we can see it is as the inevitable result of a clash of civilizations. And the way things could have gone... fifteen casualties and eighty injuries are not as catastrophic as it could have been."

"Fifteen..." said Harlowe, anguished. "That's still fifteen too many."

"I know. I'm sorry." Neil was quiet for a moment. He then pulled out the soup containers and Harlowe let out a reluctant chuckle. Neil laughed too. "I was raised to believe that this was a cure-all."

"I can see that," said Harlowe, laughing outright now.

"You'll like this, it's not that Protective Service cafeteria goop. My favourite Japanese restaurant makes an amazing miso... you'd think that it's going to be the cheap stuff at any regular restaurant but..." he shook his head, "this stuff is magic. Expensive, but magical too. But it's expensive so don't waste it," he chuckled. Harlowe accepted it graciously and they ate quietly for a while. She could barely register the taste of the soup.

Eventually she spoke.

"Alien life, you say..." The way he had framed it for her was completely novel. Especially given her job, one would think that she would be ecstatic at the thought, but it had simply escaped her all this time. She had done nothing but try not to think about anything. She would fail and inevitably she would have flashbacks to Dinar. Flashbacks to attacks. Flashbacks to her placid face on the projector screen.

"You still with us?" asked Neil casually, seeing Harlowe's far off stare.

"Uh... yeah."

"Are you looking forward to going back to work?"

"What?" Harlowe nearly spilled her soup in shock. "I... haven't even checked in with Dublin, haven't allowed anyone to come find me. Doubt I even have a job anymore."

"Oh. I guess it's too soon."

"Psssh... too soon..." Harlowe muttered. At this point she was not sure she would ever return. She had been very well-paid for her high-risk job. She did not need to return. She could retire and be ok.

"Um... should I go?" Neil looked concerned, as though he was afraid, he had upset her.

"No... I just... I wasn't prepared to think about this stuff but... it's been nearly a couple weeks, I guess I can't avoid life. I just... I don't know how people carry on after devastation. I don't even know where to begin."

"I think..." he hesitated. "I think you just do. You just take a step. And a next step. And it helps to have someone around who cares." He paused. "If you wanted... I could be that person. I could check in. I want to. You know. Being your doctor and all."

Harlowe smiled. It was funny to watch him back-pedal like that.

"Yeah," she said. "I'd like that actually."

*****

Fifty years. It had taken fifty of Harlowe's years to reach but here they were. As she and Neil climbed out of what had been their family home for the past fifty forty years and onto a firm rock surface, she felt something settle onto her chest. She was not sure what it was. Her suit was cool on her skin and she longed to hold Neil's hand in hers but settled to hold his hand through the suit's gloves.

The other two spaceships landed behind her flagship as Aaron ran out to her. Her son had spent all of his fifteen years inside the ship, sometimes in hibernation with the rest of them, other times awake, learning the basics that home-school with her and her staff could offer. All in all, a good century and a half had passed on Earth by now. Who knew what she and her fifty associates had left behind? Who knew what they had come to?

The trip had not been unanimously welcomed on Earth.

'We have enough wars here on Earth, we don't need potential enemies out in the universe too.'

'Why waste time and energy on aliens? We have enough to deal with here.'

'What's the point of risking your life for this?'

It was still an adventure worth taking and finally, after eight months of legal proceedings, Harlowe was given the go-ahead to put together a mission of trained soldiers, scientists and astronauts to embark on the adventure to seek out alien life. They had sent as many messages as they could to warn of their arrival in as many different forms as they could think.

But as Harlowe's eyes adjusted to the bright lights she looked down upon the vast emptiness. She felt confused. The last time they had checked on the coordinates it had indicated all the signs of life, a mere three months ago.

"Boss..." Andy, an eager young man who had set out immediately with a multi-purpose Measuring Device came back to report. "I think we're too late. Nuclear reading everywhere. If I didn't know any better, I'd say it was a war. Every... everything's dead. Nothing can survive on this planet."

"Are we sure this was the place? Maybe they lived --"

"This was the place, honey," said Neil. His eyes had wrinkles around them, but they were still as kind as they always been.

"So, they're all just dead..."

"Well, maybe they managed to colonize another planet like they wanted to. Maybe they're out there somewhere. But we just have to make the thirty-year journey back home now and hope that when we get there that things are all right."

Harlowe nodded but Aaron protested.

"Wait, no. We came all this way. You guys have been telling me about this day forever, we came all this way..."

"I know baby," said Harlowe. "And I am so sorry. You know, we tell you as much as we can how we never wanted this life for you, but we knew that you were our only chance to make a family. We have always wanted you to be safe and happy. We're going back on that ship, we're going to go home and when you wake up, you'll see Earth. We'll be free to start over. You'll have that life now."

He seemed set on arguing but even as he gathered his breath to protest, he released it again. There was nothing out here. With heavy footsteps they clambered back onto their ship and resigned to the thought of the long slumber to take them home.

Harlowe, Neil, and Aaron gathered with some of the crew members to watch as the planet fell into the background. The AI was running all kinds of tests to see if they missed anything but just looking at the desolate land and the craters that pocked the planet's surface, there was no doubt of what had happened here.

"Why would they do that?" Aaron asked, perplexed.

"I don't know, son," said Neil. "Sentient beings can be the most self-destructive force in the universe."

*****

They were welcomed as heroes. In telling their story, many saw it as a cautionary tale and Harlowe's words were immortalized. April 2nd, the day Harlowe's crew returned, was named Uur Remembrance Day, a day of mourning for the Uur and a day to celebrate the unity of humanity. On that day, it became common to have international differences formally resolved. These ceremonies would end with the public vow of: 'Never Again' in the hopes that humanity never wiped itself out due to war like the Uur.This is the 6 x 9 Basic Template. Paste your manuscript into this template or simply start typing. Delete this text prior to use.

www.ingramcontent.com/pod-product-compliance
Lightning Source LLC
Chambersburg PA
CBHW061340040426
42444CB00011B/3020